Her Slender Dress

Akron Series in Poetry

Winner of the 1995 Akron Poetry Prize

Susan Yuzna

Her Slender Dress

The University of Akron Press
Akron, Ohio

Acknowledgments

The Antioch Review: "The Great Divide" and "North Avenue East."
Bush Artist Fellowships Catalog: "Poem for a Redheaded Boy."
Cutbank: "Sleepless Everywhere."
The Laurel Review: "Positively Minneapolis," "The Radio," "There Are Pains Which Will Not Be Missed," and "The Way of the Moth."
Mademoiselle: "Father"
"Lake Winnibigoshish" originally appeared in *Ploughshares*, vol. 20, no.1.
third coast: "Burning the Fake Woman," "Violets."
The Best of Writers at Work, 1995: "Crossing Texas by Bus" and "The Red Fox."
Some of these poems were published in the chapbook, *Burning the Fake Woman* (GreenTower Press, 1996).
My gratitude to the Bush Foundation, especially Sally Foy Dixon, for a generosity which aided in the completion of this book.
My thanks to G. T. Wright for his good advice.
"The Way of the Moth" is dedicated to the memory of Julie Everson.

Library of Congress Cataloging in Publication Data
Yuzna, Susan, 1949–
Her slender dress / Susan Yuzna. — 1st ed.
p. cm. — (Akron series in poetry)
ISBN 1-884836-23-2 (cloth : alk. paper). — ISBN 1-884836-24-0 (pbk. : alk. paper)
I. Title. II. Series.
PS3575.U95H47 1996
813'.54—dc20 96-29135
CIP

Manufactured in the United States of America

Second printing, 1997

To the memory of
Francis Paczkowski

Contents

One

Two

Three

For the sake of a single poem, you must see many cities, many people and Things, you must understand animals, must feel how birds fly, and know the gesture which small flowers make when they open in the morning.

—Rainer Maria Rilke

One

Her Slender Dress

While the lioness
Loos'd her slender dress,
And naked they convey'd
To Caves the sleeping maid.
—William Blake

The second time
I saw Nureyev dance, I was on heroin.

It was cold in Iowa, but I was not cold
in my slender dress, gold brocade with a fringe, black,

a cheap affair, but the closest I could come
to elegance in those days. My newfound friend

kept saying, all the way over, *it's too cold, let's stay home,*
but it was really the highbrow nature

of ballet he resisted: the dancer leapt
into heaven and I would have cried

the lion's ruby tears, as I did the first time
when they handed him the roses, but heroin

allows no tears, no fluids whatsoever, you can't even pee,
so I just sighed and scratched my nose, sort of floating

in the seat as I floated on the floor
where we laid our bodies down, never

bothering to buy a bed, after shooting up together.
Needless to say, I never knew

where he was when he was beside me, when I drifted
over the arena like a gilded angel

on a cobalt ceiling, watching, with softened eye,
all the tiny people down there cheer, watching them wave

their little flags in the air, and how I loved them,
my brain's pleasure chamber humming away.

How it's not with the heart but with the brain
you follow him to the King, which is what we called heroin,

and surely it was God I felt like
with my eyes closed, serene and sexless, with the light

sparking off their sunglasses, off the watches
they encircled such delicate wrists with.

The multicolored shirts, endlessly endearing,
those silken scarves blowing in the wind. Maybe

it was a bullfight, Christians and lions, or bears.
The contest didn't matter. It was the audience I loved,

all my lively, my finely wrought creatures. And if I slipped
off my dress, *just this once,* I thought I could stay

forever, I thought I could sleep there, safe
in the ice-cold heart of a star.

The Way of the Moth

Where is there Theatre for such a fragile audience?
—Rilke

While I read late, in bed, the circumstance
of Crazy Horse's unmarked grave, the moth

drowned herself in my coffee cup. Did she
mistake the reflection of my reading lamp

for the warmth of love? Now she floats
in a pool of her unmaking, despite my resolve

to let them all live, these nocturnal visitors
slipping through screenless windows.

There really *are* tiny gold threads in her wings,
as if she wore a brocade evening gown

and on the way to the theater, collapsed.
Drowned, like tragic Ophelia. Is she really

Rilke's miniature woman, or merely one
of the insects pathologists use to fix the time

a corpse has lain in the grass, one of those
moving into the soft tissues of decaying flesh?

The magazine article I read at the beauty parlor
as my hair turned red, mentioned this fact.

Once again, in the pursuit of beauty,
the poem is drawn toward death.

A young woman, heading back to college,
had car trouble on I-80. Last seen with a phantom

truck driver thought to be a serial murderer.
Another man, stopped by the roadside near Joplin,

Missouri, covering the equipment in his pickup
truck (it was raining), found her body.

She wore a brassiere with the word *love*
embroidered between the cups, and frilly panties,

not hers, apparently provided by the murderer.
The body was already a home for insects.

Where do moths go in the rain?
Where do poems go?

I've been to Grinnell, Iowa, where she was heading,
to hear the Paul Butterfield Blues Band. I don't know

how he died, how to keep beauty in mind.
I've been through Joplin, Missouri, on a Greyhound bus,

my companion's fingers digging into my arm
as we passed the small bridge where the pickup truck

slid into the car he slept in the back seat of,
popping the driver like an egg, he said, throwing

the rest of them forward (it was raining). He held
their baby before him like a pillow (he was hitchhiking),

praying her bones would break before his did.
Later, thinking it over, he claimed to be a hero,

saving the baby's life. It makes a better story.
The gold-threaded wings of the moth

float on a surface of honey-colored coffee.
Her hair was blonde. My friend, also murdered,

was blonde. It took her a *long minute* to die,
the man answered, when asked on TV, confessing

only after acquittal, and then to save
a friend on trial. His hands wrapped tightly

around her throat. The hair, the nails, outlast
the body's soft tissue.

Shaving the Legs

He loved to watch me shave my legs.
Sitting on the toilet, he'd talk, then a quick
gasp as the blade nicked a bony place.

The skin burns, the skin objects, as when
a needle goes in the elbow's underside.
I'd offer an ankle, a knee: *here, lick the blood.*

Otherwise, an arm. Whoever goes first
offers her life. What more could he ask, I think,
each time I pull the razor over a leg, the white lotion

mounding like snow before a plow. Snow, then,
pulling myself up to the sill, standing on tiptoe.
What is this big surprise I've been promised?

Lifted by the waist, I could reach the glass
and there, over the garden, the fields, a universe
of white, curving everything. *It snowed,* he quietly said.

Touching our noses to the window, we could feel
the cold come rushing in, a violation
like steel. How hasty I was, always willing

to shoot up first, to shave fast. The snow
keeps piling up. Then wings, dropping down
from a thick rind of sky. Irresistible, are they?

Like the slim, white limbs he worshipped.
But my nose to the window, I don't feel it
long, the burning. It just keeps on snowing.

And the trees out there, feathered,
a dense white congress I am moving toward,
so dimly now, on failing wings.

Positively Minneapolis

There was a time I would have set myself on fire
for you.
But not today.
Today, the orange leaves are themselves
quite enough, placed, as they are,
into a blue sky.

Once, stepping off a ferry in Seattle
or Tacoma or wherever it was
out there where there is too much water,
where the foghorns
moan all night
as animals do when their young are taken . . .

Once, I looked up and saw you smiling
from the platform with the others
who waited for their lovers to come
sailing across the water, and I saw,
I swear,
your bones were on fire.

As I recall, the evening ended with my screwing
your friend as you watched.
I would always do what you wanted
me to do: hurt you.
Hiding in the crowd, crying out with the others,
Crucify him!

Once, the years pulled away
as smoothly as those ferries out there,
wherever it was, do.
But the last one
seemed to stop and wait, for who knows what,
huge, and burdened with light.

Through the Night

Through the night, a wire
connects me to her. She is calling
from high above Lincoln Park Zoo. In the end,
she says, we do what the animals do, we make nests.

She never liked him, she says, he was
mean-spirited from the beginning. But what I remember
is how he spread disorder behind him, like exhaust.
I know she will mention, because she's been drinking,

the blue and white room on Burlington, become
a signature with its sheer yellow curtains,
its English ivy, ruined by moonlight
but never erased. Despite the junkies

dissolving into the couch, despite the golden haze
in which we all loved each other
for a few hours, she remains
a stark, graceful form, the wineglass at ease

on the white tablecloth as a winter afternoon light falls, dimly,
from high museum windows. O, to lunch again
at the Walker, to pour out my troubles,
to be calmed by the loveliness of her face!

But now I listen, as once, on midnight shift in Oakland,
I flipped a switch, tuning back in: Manila, a young man
softly crooning to his sweetheart in Spanish.
I clocked them off, let him go on for free.

And despite the little circles lighting up
in front of my face, calls coming in from Vietnam,
Phnom Penh, Clark Air Force Base, I could not help
but listen, perched high in a fortress guarded

by day and by night from Black Panther bombs.
For him, who made me forget I was one
in a long line of tired women, for him, blooming
my 2 AM desert, for him and for her, I would stop time.

The Cheerleader

You can put down the pom-poms now, honey.
Weren't they heavy, though made of paper, like weights

lifted high, like the fireworks of his fingers, the impossible
intensity of orgasm? And your arms so skinny.

The breasts, ideally, should be full, rounding
an inflated letter nicely. You can place the rifle on the floor.

Your father safely sleeps, his head on a pillow, its border
patiently crocheted, in pastels, by your grandmother

while you watched. Remember her busy hands?
This blood mixed with brains, it looks a lot

like her berry jam. And the shrink, his white sheet
of a coat, explaining your self-esteem is low, that's why

you can't accept love from a man, he'll help you learn how—
he's gone, too. Don't your arms feel like they're floating?

Don't the birds, clearly out the window, sing a strong
three-beat line, over and over, like a cheer?

As for the roses, there, in the white vase, lift those out
and eat them, one by one, the red, red roses, while you wait.

The Radio

I still have it,
the radio you bought
that time a heroin deal
fell through, and you didn't know what
to do with the money.
It works.

I'm sitting in the basement,
listening to a man
whose job it is
to track the paths of various
tornadoes, whose job is much like
mine once was,
being your girlfriend
back in Iowa.

The radio's face is black,
trimmed with chrome,
and it has ears,
a hole in each side
where the handle was once attached
before one of us
yanked it off
during a fight.

I don't remember who,
but I get a strange and disgraceful
desire to hit you
over the head with it
just one more time, though it would be
difficult, with no handle.

I'm listening
to the flat, nasal voices
of Minnesotans
rise in pitch and velocity, for tornadoes

deeply excite us. It's as if
a cosmic sex act
flies over our heads, and we
get to watch.

We're lucky, damn lucky.
Lived here all my life.
Never seen nothin' like it.

I'm thinking
of what your psychiatrist said
after the policeman dumped you
in the detox ward
at Seattle General: *you are capable*
of anything.

Darling,
we should never have left the Midwest.

The Long Shadow

My young lover complains
he stands in line without his name.
He wants to know how many, *more than two dozen?*
O dead countrymen, O ancient governors,

what's the use? So much hoopla to the first,
in a cemetery, on a blanket, counting stars.
After, checking the mirror, my face
looked paler, surely more *womanly?*

So if, tonight, I listen
obsessively to Clapton's guitar
soar with tormented love for the wife of a friend
he gets in the end, then leaves

after she helped him kick heroin, for an Italian woman
able to bear children, and their son
falls out a window left open
on the fifty-something floor and dies, forgive me.

I listen because love really is *so sad.*
And if the man who first played this song
for me, clutching his chest
each time the guitar broke loose, its yearning

so like the human heart's, later
tried to kill me, at least I took the blues along
out the door. Was it a fair exchange?
Of course not.

But the point is, *pity,* the point is, maybe
I just wanted to wrap my legs,
my coat of mink,
around his long, hard winter.

There Are Pains Which Will Not Be Missed

I will always love you
and, like the pain in a small bone
of the foot I broke, expect your return with the rain,
with each grungy theater
I enter. *The Shadow knows*
what evil lurks in the hearts of men . . .
for the Shadow was an incredible jerk himself
back in his Butcher of Lhasa days.

I love my son more
than I will ever love you again,
and when I look over the popcorn, I see he's close
to a visionary state, his eyes Blakean, shining,
nothing like the deadly eyes
of those women in the porno flick, downtown
Chicago, as they pretended to come, repeatedly,
on the rail of a fake corral.

Dear Ghost, we're nowhere near
Chicago, where you wore
a leather jacket and rode the trains at night, high.
When you bashed my head
into the wall, the police were called
and they said, *yes, a woman out of control,*
what can you do,
take a walk next time, buddy.

Then you, off on those damn trains, snorting
with the driver, the lot
of you looping over the city, loving the way
everyone blurs into everyone else.
But if the train stops, the face
filling the window with hate
buckles my knees. *Must run.*
I know this dream.

The shudder through my body is no orgasm.
The man takes the seat next to mine
and he's huge, his face a tunnel,
the eyes weirdly receding.
How did I get on this train?
There goes the ballpark.
There goes the city line.
Yeah, yeah, all my love in vain.

Crossing Texas by Bus

I once heard a hospice nurse say that men, when dying,
recall their first time, while women speak of their children.

I had none then, crossing Texas by bus, with a man
who wanted none, it would ruin my figure, interfere

with his sex life. Possibly those endless rows of cotton,
all the white stuff erupting from pods, was what triggered

his imagination. He was like that, a poet, a collector
of experience: the time on a bus, the time on top of a ferry

crossing Puget Sound, mist in my face, tears in his eyes,
a memory like a jewel to carry with him into that violet sea.

O build your ship of death, for you will need it.
The driver, was he bored, too, piloting his forsaken bus,

going on Christmas, and if, distracted by what he saw
in his overhead mirror, he had crashed the bus, what pearls

would I be left with, fading into a bloody Texas highway,
the man beside me in bed with his Filipino whore,

so young she had no pubic hair, and cheap, less
than a dollar American. But we stepped off somewhere,

into the glare of any old terminal, and driven, always,
to seek a darkness approximating his heart, he found

a place to drink doubles, play pool. Boarding again, he spied
four young black men in the seats he insisted were ours,

the back seats, where you can stretch. Luckily for us,
I wore then, along with the water buffalo coat a rich girl

in Iowa City had given me, the perpetual stunned look
of one who'd been hit over the head and forgotten who she was.

It saved us, for after the first man said, *I don't see your name on it,*
the second, glancing my way, had mercy. *Be cool, man, we be moving,*

stay cool, he said to the crazy white boy
determined to be what my Midwestern grandfather

would call, *a hoodlum,* in these parts, *a desperado,*
escorting his new girlfriend, the lamb in water buffalo clothing,

to Arizona, where his mother, her eyes the same
dark ones he drove through this world like a phantom,

would tell her, *In this family, we have nothing*
against crazy women. But years later, she would say

I was too much the prima donna to be a wife. And it's true.
My first time on stage, age five, I noticed how the footlights

blind, no faces out there, only darkness, and you realize
how truly alone you are, so you keep the count, you try not

to fall, you imagine the many, many threads
lifting from your solar plexus, from the area of the heart,

and that is how you turn, the body slowly revolving,
a blue, blue planet in black, black space, the pull from within

versus the pull from without, *Wait, wait, the little ship,*
the balancing of it, dear ex of all Xs.

Two

Meat and Potatoes

My good German knife in hand, I begin
to peel the potatoes, and again, those Jews
of the Lodz ghetto come to mind, queued up

behind each communal kitchen, for peelings,
their doom fattening as the meat is cut
closer and closer to the skin.

In a Polish household, the man builds
into the bowels of his house a special room
for the storage of winter potatoes, grown

on the extra acre, de-sprouted by the children
before they go soft. My chore, to fetch six
each night, and I was always afraid of the room

with no light, of the possibility hidden
beneath a mountain of potatoes: some man's arm,
muscled and hairy, could reach out to grab me.

My father preached work as Rumkowski,
the Jewish godfather of the ghetto, preached it,
as salvation. The Germans need our fine tailoring,

he told them, Lodz, a textile center of Poland.
If you spoke against him, your name might appear
on the next list. My husband said, that's what was

depressing me, I read such books, *The Chronicles
of the Lodz Ghetto,* buried in a tin can
under the makeshift fire station, for future witness.

My husband said, for Christ's sake,
you're not even Jewish. But halfway through, what you
notice is the emergence of a new norm: numbers take over

the *story*, details of suicides dwindle. Just death
increasing, deportations, births reduced to near zero.
It's the new arrivals keep the numbers up.

It means they are centralizing the population
for future efficient transport. But daily business goes on.
You go to work, keep off the list. You network

with friends and family for the privilege
of collecting scraps from the back doors of kitchens
like a dog. I can't imagine it, I really can't.

My father worked at a meat-packing plant, for a Jew,
where the huge and headless bodies of steers
hung in a refrigerated room, from hooks,

like the failed assassins of Hitler, where blood
was hosed in swirls from the cement floor
into drains, and the smell, fleshy and musky, was always

horrible. My father had nothing against Jews, he said,
but thought the kosher killing cruel, to slit the throat
of a poor beast, to bleed it to death like that.

Better a quick shot to the head, he said.
And as August 1944 drew near, no potatoes,
no flour, came into the ghetto. Only cabbage and kohlrabi

arrived on the trucks. *What does it mean,* questioned
The Chronicles. On the last train to Auschwitz
rode Rumkowski and family, the letter

from a high German official finally useless.
The troops in rags, the shops shut down.
My father, in the end, believed he was a dog,

not a breadwinner. But I am still standing
over a stainless steel sink in the kitchen
of this apartment like a treehouse, high above

the commotion of transport, and from
the precise blade of the knife in my hand
dangles one long and unbroken peel.

I have done it, escaped the bad marriage.
I will eat potatoes forever. Always, the price,
I hear my friend say, as I drop the brown spiral

into the disposal and grind it to mush.
With the flip of a switch, a certain relish.
How quick, the blades. Just noise.

The Madonna, Looking Ahead

My son worries aloud
how he will get to my funeral. *I guess dad*
could give me a ride. My face, now frozen, inspires him
to add, *but first I'll stay in my room*
a long time and be sad.

I study him closely, the marble figure
in a museum's steady light. He is no longer
that thick-thighed cherub
turning, full face, from the toilet. *I don't want you to die*
like my brother's other mother did. The real one.

It begins, he is stepping out
from the composition, but, like the serious child
of the *Bruges Madonna,* holds on tightly
to a mother's thumb
while testing the smoky air with his toes.

How Michelangelo, a motherless son,
sculpted the Madonna's face
as mask, as response
to the abysmal fear of what suffering
lay ahead for her son, is astonishing.

And it is precisely because
we are so human that I take up the tools
and build, into the roof beams of his house, a memory
of the fierce love between us
so that one day, pressing

a weary forehead to the cool stone, he will know
the secret of water
pooled at the foot of the rock, timeless,
the body of the mother
become a stone church, a glass

and concrete museum, a spacious place,
the cathedral of light, sweet and vain,
falling through a window's
colored membrane.
Then, the candles smoking their grit

toward the ceiling, my supine form
between them, I will remain
in the lining of his mind, finished, a shape
familiar as the Rodin
he so admired at the Institute

we must always stop before it, his
chubby hand reaching out
from the red stroller
toward a dark and frozen movement
he recognized.

An Evening at the *Fine Line Music Café*

In the faces of my children sleep
the men who fathered them.

The faces of my children are two
silver bullets lodged in my heart,

transforming the beast. How can I ever
get this across? The tightly braided anger

loosens, falls down my back.
I watch the young woman's face.

Framed by the coatroom window,
she laughs at her half-brother's joke.

The same deep eyes as her father,
as if she sees into another world.

His high, fine cheekbones.
His shoulders so wide, I would jump off

anytime, anywhere. I can smell
his shirt yet, the one I kept in a drawer.

My son stands awkwardly, his back
to me. Large like his father, he will also

give women, by size alone, a sense
of protection. Acting tough only by direction

of his father, whose dark-skinned penis
his is a small replica of, he charms

the grown-up sister he's just met.
Tonight, I am content

to sit at a small, round table
and drink a wine from which the alcohol

has been removed. I have learned
a few things. How beauty is often

a matter of luck, not design.
How my vagina was used as a gate

through which they moved
from one world to another.

And this is exactly how I wish
to be used, my body filling

with blue light, wide as a sky
over mountains. But hush, now,

the singer appears. He sits down
at the piano. Yes, there will be many

joining us tonight. Many ghosts
whose footprints remain in the snow of the heart.

And the singer, he's older, too, still claiming
to know what love is.

The Great Divide

Some of us get across.
Now rivers run the other way.
The towns are filled with casinos, pawn shops.
Now I don't buy, I sell.
My grandmother's fire opal
for thirty-five dollars. A blond boy
once told me, jumping a fence
(me in a bikini, he in jeans and cowboy boots),
it was bad luck
wearing an opal when it wasn't your stone.
We tore up the dusty road
in his light blue convertible
but made it to Happy Hour on time, arriving
already half-drunk, and my bikini, did it
drive them mad. I know.
Forgive me.

Oh, Jeffrey. Each evening I walk out the door
of my little house here
in Missoula, to see if the world is still there.
Half-drunk on stars, the moon
fixed above Mount Jumbo.
Inside, a boy sprawled on the floor
before a TV, a dog asleep
on the couch, love me very much.
And you, still a boy, jumping the fence
with a grin, arguing the merits of Tanqueray
gin. I watch you striding down the road
in jeans unwashed for weeks.
Southern Iowa steamed.
Sexy as hell
from behind.

The men dumping you on a stretcher
didn't think so. One,
looking down, unlike

the moon, said, *you junkie*
piece of shit.
Or so I was told, later,
by faces blank as moons,
gathered in a room
hushed as that evening in the mountains
when I stopped at a rest area
near the Divide
to pee and let the dog run,
when a bird hovered
just over my head.
My son said, *don't move.*
The mountains grew bluer,
the moon a gracious
white sphere. Only the wind
knows us.

North Avenue East

for my son

Opening the front door of this cottagelike house
to find the sky full of stars and clouds streaming by
startles me every time, like falling in love,
when suddenly you see just how deep and wide

the man is. A day of snow melting in Minnesota,
an occasion for checking the oil. Glancing up from under
the hood of my old Thunderbird, I saw in the green
eyes of your future father, a passion strong as you have become:

balanced astride his bike, there on the sidewalk
in front of his house, like an apparition, electrifying. How can I
explain? I see him as if through water now. What catches your breath
is the swiftness, becoming a stranger to what you knew

as the natural order. The night you were born, the world
was reduced to the metal buckle of your father's belt.
I could endure the pain only by hanging on to what I knew.
Eye level, the belt loop of his jeans, as the current swept me

toward oblivion. I understood no words until he repeated
what the doctor said, what the nurse said. Now the words
lie deep within the blue spruce that looms from our neighbor's
yard. You tell me you remember watching us bend

toward each other and kiss, one Fourth of July,
as fireworks over the Mississippi flared
in the window behind us. What else
can we do, against the black window, but shine?

To the Moon Over the Mountain

They say you are old hat.
On TV tonight, they claim you were conquered
by the men sitting there, white-haired now,
lightly bouncing off your body
in their thick-soled boots
like boys on a trampoline.

Twenty-five years ago
and what do we know about the nature of anything?
There was a saint, once, claimed
more demons work between us and the moon
than move through the entire rest of the cosmos.
Saint Jerome, I think it was.

But what I know is
when you let loose your fullness
and allow me no sleep, I must leave my house.
I must walk around and around
the door of the beloved,
for mystics have said

it is most foolish
to presume entry: a ferocious, white fire.
That shadow on the wall
was once a person
walking forward, hand outstretched.
Once a person coming toward you.

Scanning for Christ

It seems
everyone is scanning for Christ
of late, in the laundromat, on the next
subway seat, behind fresh seafood at Safeway.
Is that him,
a parcel tucked under his arm, crossing
the bridge? Look how the light
envelops his head, how he continues
through fields of unbroken snow,
leaving no prints.

Beware the man who claims
to be enlightened. He will distress you,
fault your housekeeping, call that child of yours
unruly. Beware the man
claiming ethics for his father, as if he would inherit
a genetic trait. I dream of the fathers,
heavier, now, around the middle,
their wives still pulling out the scrapbooks
to show those World War II photos: here he is
in uniform, lean, smiling.

I should have been his daughter
by marriage, offered my son to the clan.
Severely, he says, *it's about time*
I saw you again. It must be Sunday morning.
He's gone to make pancakes as usual.
But I am a Venus in sackcloth.
I am the Magdalene
finding her other body parts
just as useful. Did he tell you that, together,
we have seen the evening's far places?

Besides, it's the pissed-off Christ I like, the red-faced
young man throwing the moneychangers out.
He sits down to consider the elm.

I know who he is
and he is no hero. It's such a relief
between us. And if I smoke a cigarette, here,
under the elm's green awning, waiting
his intention, he won't mind.
You know what I mean.
We give ground.

On the Way to Lolo Hot Springs

If I wrapped myself in some animal's skin,
wore one silver earring
and smoked opium,
it would embarrass him. If I wandered
over the desert, whirling
and whirling until my spirit broke through
the veil of the actual, he would say
he wants a *traditional* mother, lingering
over the word with a nostalgia
incredible for his ten years.

He finds the trees boring.
The mountains don't move him,
nor does my account of Lewis and Clark
threading their way through this canyon.
He is thoroughly engaged
in moving a minuscule blue hedgehog
over a two-inch screen
by pushing buttons, collecting
rings of power, exploding boxes.
The desert would be quiet.

In the photograph
I keep thinking of, a Pakistani woman
leans against the brick wall
opposite a saint's tomb, her long, black hair
splayed over the crumbling surface
as if electrified. Thin as sin, and deep
into the trance, while a child
beside her sleeps, his round rump
barely covered. I could live
on locusts and honey.

Burning the Fake Woman

On 1 June 1310 in Paris at the Place de Grève, a beguine, referred to as a "pseudo-mulier," was burned at the stake as a relapsed heretic, having written a book "filled with errors and heresies."

She won't apologize
for running loose in the world,
claims a direct line to God.
Thus, the crusty old farts
become peripheral, their blueprint
for salvation, inferior, the old boy
network, irrelevant. *Jesus*
on that mainline—
all you need is love.

They burn her alive.
But they warn you first,
don't they? The Bishop of Cambrai,
burning her book in public,
forced her to watch.
The book won't die.
It lives on, underground,
passed from hand to hand.
Call in William

of Paris, the Dominican inquisitor,
who throws her in jail
with Guiard de Cressonessart, a beghard
who pledged himself
to her defense.
O what happens to the man
supposed to be your bulwark?
A year and a half
under major excommunication,

he breaks,
confessing to his mission

as the Angel of Philadelphia,
trading the flames
for life in prison. The woman
still won't talk, *suspected of heresy,*
in rebellion and insubordination
. . . would not respond before the inquisitor
to those things pertaining to the office of inquisitor.

Silence or confession,
either way, she's fucked.
Like the Templars before her,
she must roast, but this time
in the middle of town,
no suburban field for her,
so all can watch, and learn
the formidable power of
the office over the woman.

And here we sit, all these
centuries later, at the edge
of Missoula, Montana,
watching a *pseudo-mulier,*
a truly fake woman,
being passed around the bar.
Filled with air, undressed,
a black garter and stockings
painted onto her vinyl body.

Two slits in the crotch,
a vagina and an anus.
How nice to have a choice,
Judy says, as we gaze past our beers,
witness to Herod, or Jared and Duane,
drunk and singing karaoke
from the stage. A big screen
to their right plays out the scene:
a cowgirl lassoing

her too-handsome cowboy
in the fairyland corral.
A perfectly round ball
bouncing up there on the screen
rests a moment
over each word
I'm supposed to sing—
lies, lies, flashing by so fast
I think they may be flames, yes, flames.

Violets

For if you are alone you are completely yourself but if you are accompanied by a single companion you are only half yourself.
—Leonardo da Vinci

Possibly you saw him standing alone,
drink in hand, eyes shot through with a hunger
men never lose. So you take him home, though
you don't really mean it, you tell yourself.
Soon enough, you navigate the blizzard
toward his house, cars in the ditch, each covered
with a thick shroud. O haven't you yet learned,
traveling through the cold country for ten
thousand years, the key is to keep moving,
to never, but never, stop, to refute

the wool shawl his dead wife left, to resist
picking up that first violet, lonely
in the supermarket, stuck there among
fruits and vegetables, inconsolable
in the stark light. Soon, you are depending
upon a purple chorus, they shine so,
the blossoms, deep and fluted, rather like
vaginal lips, the leaves thrusting upwards,
thick-veined, reaching for the filigreed light
lace curtains allow. Erasmus Darwin

understood this sexual property
of flowers, his book eroticizing
their functions thought to have influenced Blake's
treatise on Female Ruin. The Lily
speaks to Thel, but to no avail, for when
the Virgin hears a voice breathe the endless
why from her own grave, she jumps up and flees.
And if Darwin's grandson, Charles, saw it
always in terms of warfare, wasn't this
the essential difference between us?

The Junkyard

I constructed a family
from secondhand items: baby
carriage wheels, adding machines,
things gathering dust in back rooms.
Make the best of it, they told me.

Once started, there is no stopping it.
Always, the unseen variable.
So I gave the firemen the okay:
go in with your axes.
Stop it at any cost.

Looming, for a glorious instant, white
against the evergreens
massed together like a prayer,
their roots secret, and wet,
it went down.

The orchestra played on.
Our pleas went ignored.
We drifted on dark water.

Sometimes, I think it is done.
Then I think of the next man.
Serenely, in the evening, I stroll with my dog
through rusted shapes
as the sun drops down.

But where is the junkyard man
who asks no questions,
who knows better
than to mess with a lady's poison?
Listen, the three low notes

that never stop sounding.
Over an elegant line
of horizon, like hell hounds, they keep coming.

Draw near, my shadow, be steel.

The Way of the Moth II: At an Amtrak Station

Behind glass, a large man stands, smoking,
waiting for a train, for a son, for Christmas.

Biologists studying an orange and black moth
found that a female will mate with more than one male

and then actively select from the various offerings
the sperm of the biggest male she has dallied with.

He won't see us, the windows tinted blue
against the glare. He never smoked when we were

married. *Female moths engage in promiscuous sex*
to gather the desirable defense chemicals and nutrients

that accompany the male's sperm during intercourse.
We pass through the glass. The boy waits for a sign

from this large man. They stand together awkwardly,
without purpose. *To demonstrate that he is endowed*

with a generous spermatophore, the courting male
will extrude from his head brushes scented with a whiff

of the defensive alkaloid, and lightly whisk the little
brushes against the female. I watch them disappear,

in search of a Coke machine, and I know the boy won't dare
speak his heart for two weeks; already he accommodates

the longer stride. *If she agrees he is properly furnished,*
the female allows the male to mount her and ejaculate

the spermatophore, a considerable feat. I suppose
I expected more: the strength of a giant, the courage

of a hero. *The spermatophore in these moths is huge.*
It's 11 percent of the male's body mass. The man's

immigrant grandfather, Slovenian, wore a handlebar
mustache. To prove his manliness, to stand up

to the miners' jeers, those Finns, those Italians,
he went down with the men. *It's equivalent*

to a 180-pound man having a 20-pound ejaculate.
Two weeks later, the mine collapsed, leaving

a woman with eight children, no survivor's
benefits, a ham at Christmas. *The female*

detects the largest male because the largest
male also makes the largest spermatophore.

The boy, walking away, his stride lengthening,
(the man won't slow) will grow to be large also.

The hefty packet in turn stretches the genital
canal, a distention that is in a sense memorized

by the female. Knowing the relative mass
of her paramours, the female can choose

which sperm to channel toward her eggs
by appropriate squeezing of the muscles,

diverting unsavory sperm toward side chambers
along the way. When they return to me, waiting

at the glass door with the luggage, smoking,
the boy is remote. *Dr. X, who was the first*

to suggest that females might engage
in post-copulatory selection of sperm,

said the strategy was likely to be widespread
in the animal kingdom. The boy is struggling

with a heavy suitcase, while the man carries two,
three, easily. I'm following in their wake, free

of weight. In the cold air, I can almost hear
a symphony of twitching brushes.

Three

Poise

It was February, damn cold
when I stood over him.
His skin had collapsed over the bones.

Looking so thin, propped up
against the puffed satin cushions
of the casket. I thought, how much air

must be in us, how much water.
His hair combed straight back, oiled,
his hooked Polish nose

jutting out like the prow of a sunken ship.
My sister screamed and ran.
Later, my arm around her,

we sat on a small velvet sofa,
deep red, as the sobs
moved all the way up her body.

I sat mute, helpless, a stone
on the very bottom.
It was mistaken for poise.

Off to the Legion, where you drink
a lot of drinks. You play pinball,
pool. You listen to your aunt tell everyone

how weird you were as a child.
You remember the booths of dark leather,
smooth, cold to the touch.

The long banquet tables, lonely,
with no people talking. And on the wall
hung a black-and-white photograph:

the young sailor smiling at you,
a white cap way back on his head
the way sailors wear them.

How many times did you read the story
typed on heavy, white paper
beneath the photo: how the radioman,

only nineteen, went down with his ship,
how he kept calling for help
as the water filled her up.

How many times did you stand there
facing him, it must have been
a hundred, rereading the details

of his heroic death, waiting, it seemed,
forever, for your father
to pick up his money and drive you home.

Father

It is the dead,
Not the living, who make the longest demands.
—Sophocles

You once said you saw
a stripper right here

in this city, looked just
like me, as young, and you

thanked your stars I was home
safe, but here I am,

old man, with the bugs
in my drink heading for the

invisible shore, and here
I am, dead man, drunk

just like you, starless,
and here I am.

O Canada

In the cry of the geese flying over, I heard him.
The old ones have come. This time they don't

turn their smooth shining faces around
when he comes to, a doctor bending over,

deputies behind, sheepish, in trouble for
forgetting his belt. Too quiet, they thought,

for a drunk Indian. Not his time, he said then,
but I'm left standing on ice-encrusted grass,

the black *V* slicing through, and I'm left
standing that day in class, proofing their typing.

I turn the Stones up, so loud the girls all giggle,
the teacher frowns. *You can't say we're satisfied* . . .

The Human Relations lady wishes to speak
with me. And I'm left standing in the empty

classroom, my back to a long row of windows.
I can't hear what she's saying, for more geese

are coming, and in my fatigue, her tall form,
dressed in office-appropriate black, wavers

as though she's underwater. The geese
grow so loud I turn around, expecting them

into the room, but no, they head the other way,
and it sure looks like some kind of paradise

where they go. Her voice, low, is coming through,
she's saying I'm a special person. I turn back,

she's rippling. I try to focus on this raven
of a woman, her arms very long, held close.

A *very special person. I just wanted to tell you.*
She walks out then and I return to the window,

to the precise constellation of birds,
the momentum of them, lucky in the sky.

At the Division of Vocational Rehabilitation, I Learn I Am Not Human

Playing the piano
no longer fills these enormous afternoons.
My audience left. His lovely long legs
went with him. I'm no master
but he listened. Standing
beyond a door, in the jaundiced air
of a tiled hall, he just *listened.* How little
we require, after all.

Covering the keys, I will pay my visit
to the oak and brick haven.
The young man makes me wait
long enough to understand
I am refuse
deposited upon his shore, and he,
the Savior. I notice his suit
is badly cut, wrinkled, definitely discount.

They must not pay much. He explains
the procedure, eyes fixed on the table,
though it's mighty flat
like the land you see go on forever
beyond a window here. A few oaks,
quite old and spectacular,
a metaphor for the stability
they are so proud of.

He returns, a new man, to inform me
I have the highest score
in the history of the place
on the verbal comprehension test,
beating even his. Where did I *take* my degree,
he asks me. I see, now we are colleagues.
You're too consistent to be human.
He smiles. *You're off the graph.*

It appears I answered each
repeated question
the same way every time
when I'm expected to change my mind.
We aliens . . .
those patients, for instance, I can see
out the window, heading for
the meal line, the MIs drugged on Thorazine

who pour their milk so slowly—
the dumpy woman who always sits
in a corner, all alone,
reputedly the whore of the place—
word is, they meet in distant trees for sex.
Where else can we find
answers so reliable
as tall trees in the bluest of evenings?

Grace, and the Lack Of

In the motel, I forgot to tell
him he was mistaken: I'm not a cardinal, but a dove.

I forgot entirely, turning thirty, the man, Ojibwa,
and we faced the wrong way, astride the gate

of someone else's station wagon. There was a lot
to laugh about: counselors who needed counseling,

the newest fools dropped into the net. But the light
was soft, pale, an evening in June, dust rising

from gravelled roads. For years, it's been
too dry, too wet. On TV, you could see

the farmers' sons water-ski over their fields.
Luckily for my grandfather, he's dead and buried

next to his beloved corn. The consequence
of this uncertain weather would surely reduce him

to Norwegian nonsense. *Feesh, fee da.*
Them Nelson boys, they went wild, left the farm.

Now just look at it. Good for nothin'.
But there comes a breeze, a mercy, and the hills,

gentle, too, here in this corner of the state
the glaciers missed, where the Mississippi

bends to the east. A few hills on the plains
make everyone happy, and so shall we

by making our three meetings a week.
At the priests' retreat, he shows me the painting.

A dove flees the pursuing hawk. *That's you,*
he says, *that's me.* The priests begin

a new litany: how they drank until dawn, a toast
to each saint, there's enough of them, then first light

cracks, but the Spirit, still silent, on a faraway branch.
Isn't loss of faith the real issue? Must you flee

in your scarlet tunic, the white antelope
circling? Will you call from Wisconsin?

Step sideways into the trees?
Or run naked down Fourth Avenue

as a man did one afternoon, arms held high,
the muscles of his buttocks pumping away.

It took six big men to hold him down. He was
screaming, no, it was more like moaning, the sound

rising from a well of terror possibly brilliant somehow
and blinding, like sunlight on fresh snow, the male

cardinal's blood-color against a soft curve
of thigh, I mean, snow, the nest

of blood in a beaten-down snowbank
where a dove once walked, her demeanor,

the man with a walkie-talkie, his desire
to report a location, his need of aid.

In the crowd where I stood, a woman
continued to fan her face with the newspaper.

It happens now and then, she said.
And the hawk? I lost him somewhere

in Wisconsin. Chippewa Falls? Rice Lake?
The rain so quick, so hard, I had to pull over

to recover. And the motel, its goings-on
will remain mysterious as the dove's demeanor,

the American kestrel's habit of nesting
in holes abandoned by others, feeding, mating,

on the same perch, unlike us, that summer I found him
already among the trees, unyielding.

Poem for a Redheaded Boy

A boy lost somewhere
between fat and muscle, he knew only
how to speak with his body. Sitting
on my stomach is what he favored,
grinning a goofy, desperate love
over my prostrate form.

Though flat on my back in the grass—
don't expect this poem
to turn sexual. It's about *trust,* about ducking
under our desks when the air raid siren blew,
believing our parents and teachers knew
how to save us

from nuclear vaporization, about the pure
redemption of his home run swing—the small moon
of a baseball as it hung
in the blue sky over a cornfield—
how I see him yet, in a sky over Vietnam
he was blown out of.

How evening would surprise us
by falling suddenly,
and always, at the end, the mothers would appear,
one by one, at their back doors,
and they are calling out our names,
the moon a crescent,

the stars sharpening, and we are picking up
our gloves, we are moving faster
through weeds, through gravel,
the smell of cut grass—then, blooming
from the night, our own
high and lighted windows.

The Red Fox

I might as well be on the moon
as in Brooklyn Park. Flat, white. I'm talking
Minnesota, in February. It's so cold,
the wheels of the car *clonk*.
Why have I come back?

Apparently, to drive around in circles.
At the University, they have built a bookstore
into the ground on the same principle
my ancestors used: heating efficiency.
Dug into the prairie in caves, sod-roofed,

against the long winters, against the Sioux
expelled from Minnesota
after the final war, the thirty-eight
Santee leaders hanged at Mankato,
a cold dawn, the day after Christmas,

in the largest mass execution
of American history, though Lincoln
did pardon some hundreds. Facing west,
holding hands, they sang to the death
approaching. Questions remain,

but the men in my family
don't ask questions when land is free:
this is not Poland. The men in my family
drink all day and through the night.
I saw one jump off a table,

flapping his arms, trying to fly.
The whole next day, not a word.
Then he plowed half the night.
They use lights. Still, it's dangerous.
They say it's the only way to profit from wheat.

The men in my family go to church
only Christmas and Easter.
Snow begins falling. I'm in
the Buick with my father,
it's forty years ago, and we're stopped

at the intersection where a massive
Christmas tree is placed each December.
He's swearing, fogging the windows.
They should take that thing down.
A goddamn danger to traffic.

The bells from Saint Theodore's
begin ringing the hours
for midnight Mass.
The bells, the bells,
swinging their hips.

Perhaps only my reverence will save me,
writes the Polish poet exiled to America.
But my brother's new wife is American,
Indian, and lost in the suburb
much like an orphaned red fox

some hunters once gave him. Later,
released into the woods, she came back.
We threw apples, then stones,
but she stayed, and as my brother knew
they would, the dogs took after her.

Hiding under our car, she drove them frantic.
My brother ran into the house,
came out with his rifle and shot her.
We burned the body in our garden,
my brother disappearing into the woods,

as he often did, so no one could see him cry.
We just stood there, without words,
staring at the charred mess of her,
truly amazed
by this love story.

The Engine Upon Which We Depend

Driving
my niece to the mall, this girl
whose heart is in the wrong place, we pass condos
built over a pond I once skated on. I could tell her

there was no warming house, tell her
my brother is calling across the slick oval of ice
from clumps of frozen cattails, *just keep moving,*
you'll stay warmer that way.

I could tell her the horses
named for my favorite books
loped to the fence when they saw me
drop my bike and walk toward them, fist closed

over the bribe. Their large, easy eyes
held secrets I needed to know. But the horses
could not have saved her, could only look down
and neigh, the sounds soft as moths

fluttering over a dusky-skinned baby
whose heart beat on the right rather than left
side of her chest, a hole in it big enough
for a moth to fly through.

A large and shiny building saved her,
men in green clothing and masks,
tissue from a human corpse
harvested for rewiring a heart grown wrong.

What you notice in the nursery
is how quiet it is, babies hooked up to tubes,
too drugged to move. Critical Care nurses
cut diapers the size of Kleenex

to fit the tiny butts. And when it's terribly quiet,
they "lost one" overnight. If you listen

to the doctors, as my sister did, what you hear
are the odds, 50/50, on the table.

Thirteen years later, I buy her lunch at the mall,
after she's shown me the jacket
she's saving her money for,
sure to make her too cool for school.

Idolizing Madonna, she wears a filmy blouse
over the scars which curve from her neck
down over her chest and around
to her back. Her lips, the moons

of her fingernails, no longer blue. I could tell her,
but I'm sure she remembers
the boys on the same floor of Saint Mary's
that last open-heart, the boys wandering the halls,

their bare heads covered with string
and paper hats, were terminals
with inoperable brain tumors.
One, at a small table, played checkers

with his mother. His skin, green, his mother,
utterly calm. This girl, wheeled into surgery,
smiled at her mother, said, *don't worry.*
Now, she asks to buy my car

when she's old enough. She has no intention
of wasting her time. I show her how
to shift into reverse. The sun glints
off the mall's green roof.

Above, I watch the horses come toward us.
I'm tired, I tell her, *of my leather jacket.*
Do you want it? There,
I've made the girl smile.

Lament of a Non-Native

To the memory of
Margaret Brunsvold Grandokken

A cowgirl I am not.
In the country I come from, a tree is an event.
I've never even seen a grizzly, but for
the illustration on a comic book cover
my brother once carefully lifted

from the revolving wire rack of the Northside Confectionery:
Daniel Boone, midstream, somewhere in the wilderness,
his trusty knife raised over his head.
It was the very moment
before he would stab her in the heart.

How did I know the bear was female?
I just knew
and still, I sided with Daniel, filching
my brother's fake raccoon-tail hat
every chance I got.

So when I opened the box to find
not the expected pathfinder's hat, but a blouse
(puffed-up sleeves, tiny heart-shaped rhinestone buttons),
I said, *this is not a hat, this is not*
what I wanted, if you please.

I was sent to my room for being rude to my grandmother
who, as an old woman, striding toward the chickens,
waved the long, thin arms
which were like wings as they emerged
from her faded, cotton apron. *Shoo, shoo, out*

of the garden! Out! Maggie, the schoolmarm,
keeping up the argument,
part English, the swear words, Norwegian,

and those hens, backed off
to the fence, furious, still bitching.

On the very next occasion, she presented me
with the hat, and how like a charm
it worked: the woods turning wild, thick
as the gray smoke of her eyes
in the nursing home, where she reverted, completely, to Norwegian.

Lake Winnibigoshish

The trees, so white and so many.
I don't remember it this way.
Their slender trunks a comfort.

You surrender, that's all.
To a man, to a drug, to wall after wall
of birch. It's not unpleasant.

Winnie, steel-gray in October.
Whitecaps. This is where
nostalgia will take you: a mean wind,

a sleety snow pricking your face.
Turn the car around,
head west.

A thin snow already covers the ground
of the clearing. Two small buildings,
WOMEN and MEN, on the far side.

I stop and look up.
I don't know why.
The tops of the trees are spinning.

How does the wind manage this?
How do I hear my name
when no one is here?

This much I know: a skinny white woman
stands in the snow.
Tell me the rest.

At the Cass Lake E Z Stop, I find
a T-shirt pinned to the wall:
Where Eagles Soar.

I don't remember eagles here,
just my father saying, *God,*
look how they live,

as we passed through,
four kids and a dog
in the back seat of a Buick.

Eagles, hawks, doves.
I never quite understood the stories.
From around here, the Bear Clan.

Like the bear, we scare people.
Scared ourselves, we turn
and run into the woods.

I buy the T-shirt with its awful
green lettering. It's what I know.
Purchase. Surrender.

History: Real, Invisible

It strikes me as utterly appropriate
they now sell high-priced denim outfits
over the very spot
where you beat me up

and ruined everything. There is
no argument
strong as the need of returning.
Many criminals do it.

Like Judas Iscariot, I pause
at the edge of a small wall
and smoke a cigarette, movielike,
while considering the inevitable

nature of betrayal. The cock
must crow, be sure of it, and bits
of silver will shine
from the darkness like daggers.

Yet, it's hard, amazingly hard,
to give up a secret I've carried
too long. Twenty years? But it pours
rain, always a mercy

in this oven of a town,
so I take off my shoes, tuck my legs up
under a long skirt, as in the days
when National Guardsmen

patrolled these streets, so young
and scared out of their wits
they'd have to shoot someone.
We'd just exited a theater.

The Godfather was playing,
remember? *Go home, please,*

a loudspeaker pleaded.
Your parents don't want you in jail.

In Rome, they built Bramante's
new Saint Peter's
right over the old one—the Popes
were not known for patience, nor reverence.

Who would remember the past?
It grows small, and seems
so odd now, like waking from a dream
in which you wore a clown's mask

and were running away
from a bloodied corpse. How did I know
it was you, masked as you were,
the nose grown magically

long as Pinocchio's, and why did I
think of that horrible carrot-nose
the rapist in *A Clockwork Orange* used
as he went about the business of atrocity

while singing a cheery song?
You see, it was the fear
I recognized in your fleeting form, that
inexplicable terror that has always propelled you.

Stopping at Wind Cave

The land rolls away in all directions. A few buffalo.
Bison, my son corrects me. He can be such a shit

when he knows something I don't. But I know
this is where The People came out

from the earth, from the longest running cave
in a circle of caves, from the absence of fire,

the earth's belly cooling, and the Hills settled into
a blue-black mystery. A wind snake winding

through miles upon miles of empty, dark womb.
I feel this hunger, too, for a new vista.

The water table's fallen, due to the drought,
the Ranger says. No mention of mining,

nor the rest. We descend in an elevator
built by the WPA. He turns the lights out

to show us what true darkness is. My son
holds tightly to my hand. The cave is constantly

adjusting to the upper atmosphere—thus, wind
is born. And though we stand, now, in total

darkness, I know he stands beside me
and I know this is where The People came out

from The Mother, rising like breath from her lungs,
crawling through a small hole hidden in rock,

startled by the light, by mountains steady
as a father's shoulders, by the whole panorama

of creatures, flying and walking. *Sister, brother.*
If you wish to speak, we are listening.

Sleepless Everywhere

Who are those clouds flying by,
the doves, the doves at their windows?
Ezekiel said (something like that).

And Crazy Horse supposedly said,
it's a good day to die, or someone did.
He went for days without sleep,

without food, to enter his vision.
The horseman came to him, rode on.
Soldiers fell out of the sky

for another. They kept falling,
the horses, the soldiers,
though the window stayed open

and stepping through it
was confusing, said the brother
who betrayed him, as Judas

would agree. There was a man
worked for God and the Borgia devil
by turns, Leonardo da Vinci,

sleeping fifteen minutes
every four hours, then rising
to attach paper wings

to small, green lizards. Nowhere
in his voluminous notebooks
is there mention

of human affection. How can you
not love the man?
Salvador Dali napped

sitting upright, a spoon
balanced on his palm.
The noise of its dropping woke him.

None of it works for me.
An ordinary sort of insomniac,
I watch out the window.

Who are those stars twirling by
in their white, white dresses?
Weren't we pretty then?

Except for the Smith girl, an angel,
my father said she looked like,
laid out in her white dress and veil.

The car cresting a hill
just as she forgot to look, as swift
and unimaginable as eternity.

O Mary, Mary, quite contrary,
if you came back
in your white dress and wings,

would I stop being afraid at night?
If you came to the swings
of Saint Theodore's

black-topped playground
after First Communion class,
we could tell secrets again

(I like your panties)
as the wind passes, cool
and pleasing, between our thighs.

And to show how I love you,
I would pump harder
over the hills of air,

I would hang upside down
in the posture of Saint Peter
on his cross, my feet

pointed to heaven:
a slow crucifixion
the more glorious.

O Ezekiel, strangled by his wheel,
and grandpa, drunk on 7 Crown,
these fierce old men,

I don't want them.
Give me a hand, a soft one,
to place on the forehead of fever.

A man like a mother.
Let the dove go.
Let the angel fall silent.

Surrounding Leonardo's
effeminate Saint John the Baptist
is a darkness you've never seen,

out of which the boy-prophet
smiles. The final gesture,
his signature, a finger

pointing up and away
from the slight self.
His cross, a slender thing.

Notes

Burning the Fake Woman

1. *Pseudo-mulier* means, literally, "fake woman."

2. Epigraph is from Ellen L. Babinsky's introduction to *The Mirror of Simple Souls* by Marguerite Porete.

3. Fourth stanza quotes the second deliberation against Marguerite Porete, May 9, 1310.

The Way of the Moth II: At an Amtrak Station

Entomological information is from "May the Best Moth Win," *Minneapolis Star Tribune*, 6 June 1993.

ABOUT THE AUTHOR

A Bush Writing Fellow in 1995, Susan Yuzna has a BA in English from the University of Iowa and an MFA in Creative Writing from the University of Montana, where she was a Richard Hugo Memorial Poetry Scholar. Ms. Yuzna teaches English at the University of North Dakota.

ABOUT THE BOOK

Her Slender Dress was designed and typeset on a Macintosh in Quark XPress by Kachergis Book Design of Pittsboro, North Carolina. The typeface, Electra, was designed in 1935 by William Addsion Dwiggins. It is a standard book typeface because of its evenness of form and its high legibility.

This book was printed on sixty-pound Natural Hi-Bulk and bound by Braun-Brumfield, Inc., Ann Arbor, Michigan.